PIANO · VOCAL · GUITAR

HAL·LEONARD
WEDDING ESSENTIALS
INCLUDES REFERENCE CD

COUNTRY
WEDDING FAVORITES

ISBN 978-1-4234-9920-6

HAL·LEONARD®
CORPORATION
7777 W. BLUEMOUND RD. P.O. BOX 13819 MILWAUKEE, WI 53213

For all works contained herein:
Unauthorized copying, arranging, adapting, recording, Internet posting, public performance,
or other distribution of the printed or recorded music in this publication is an infringement of copyright.
Infringers are liable under the law.

Visit Hal Leonard Online at
www.halleonard.com

T0087251

COUNTRY
WEDDING FAVORITES

AMAZED

Words and Music by MARV GREEN,
CHRIS LINDSEY and AIMEE MAYO

Moderately slow Country Ballad

*Recorded a half step lower.

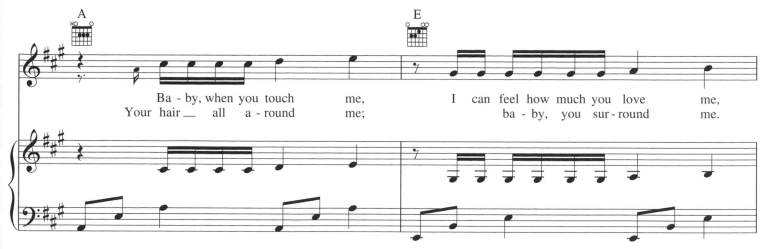

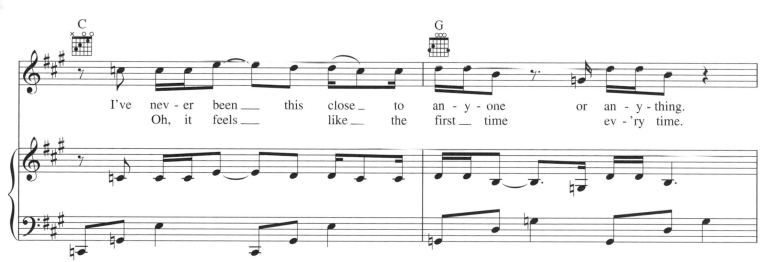

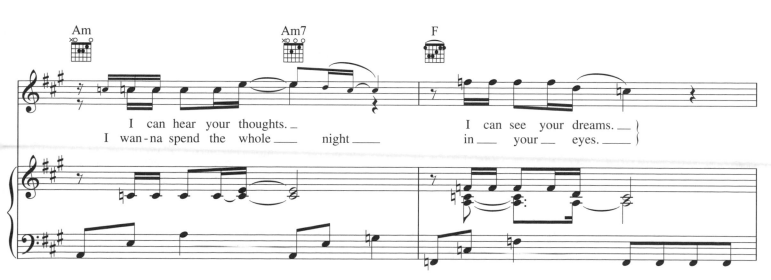

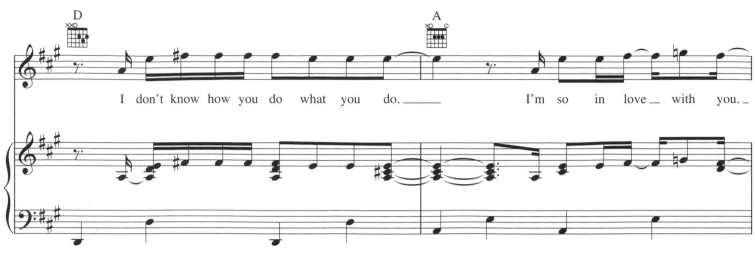

I don't know how you do what you do. ____ I'm so in love __ with you. __

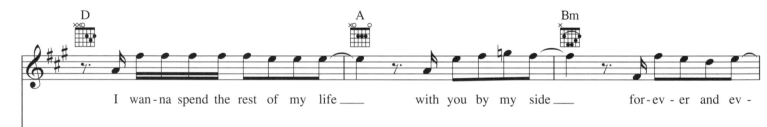

____ It just keeps get-tin' bet - ter.

I wan-na spend the rest of my life ____ with you by my side ____ for-ev - er and ev -

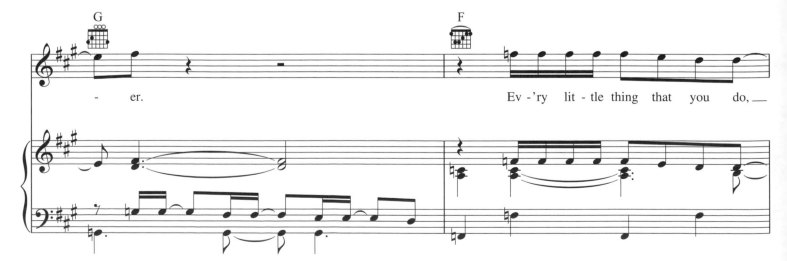

- er. __ Ev -'ry lit - tle thing that you do, __

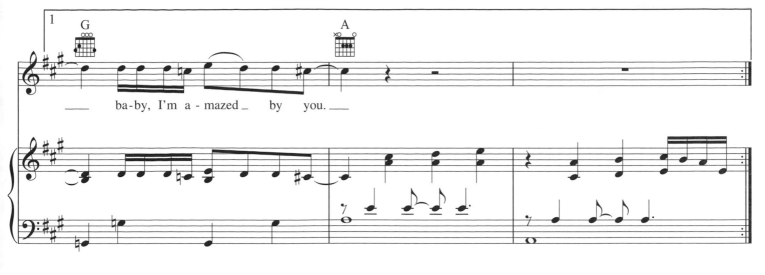

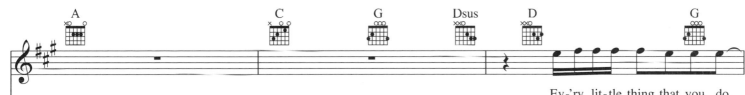

I wan - na spend the rest of my life _____ with you by my side _____

_____ for-ev-er and _ ev - er. Ev-'ry lit-tle thing that you do, _

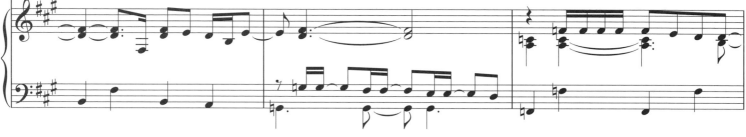

_____ oh, _____ ev-'ry lit - tle thing that you _ do, _

Freely   **Tempo I**

_____ ba-by, I'm a-mazed _ by _ you.

I SWEAR

Words and Music by FRANK MYERS
and GARY BAKER

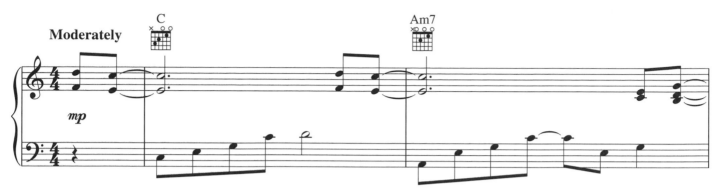

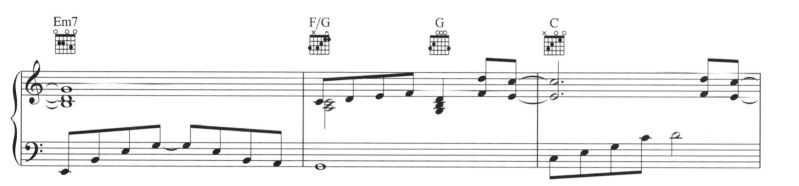

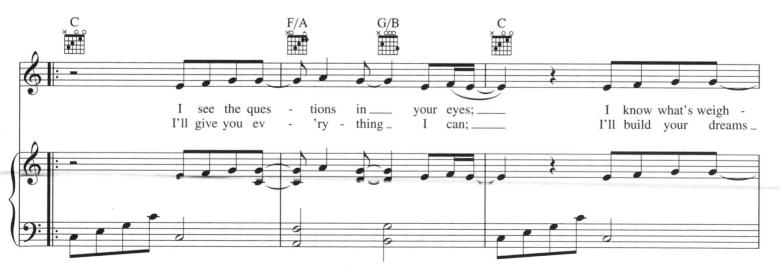

I see the ques - tions in ___ your eyes; ___ I know what's weigh -

I'll give you ev - 'ry - thing ___ I can; ___ I'll build your dreams ___

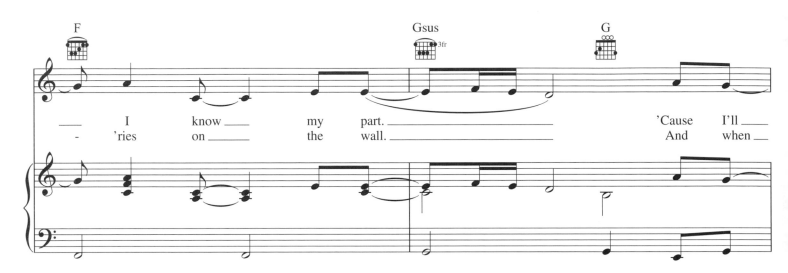

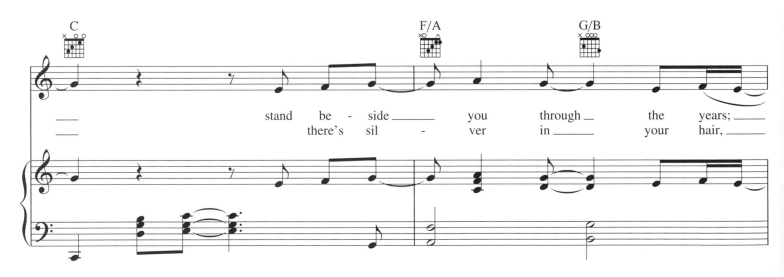

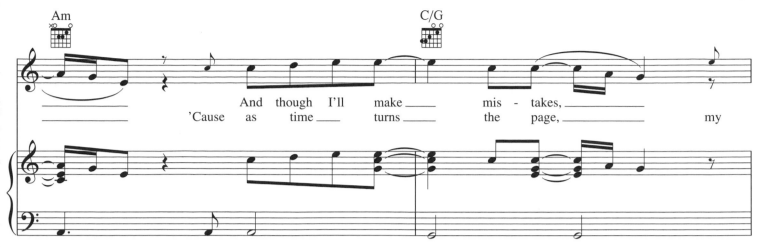

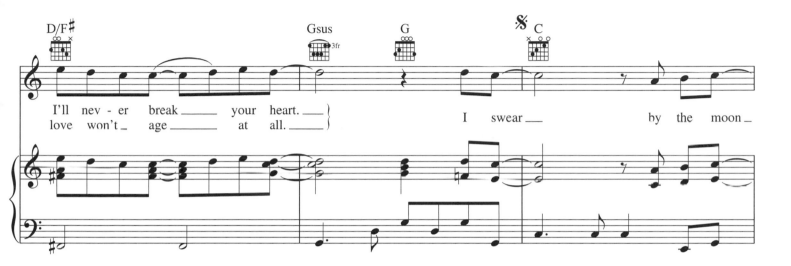

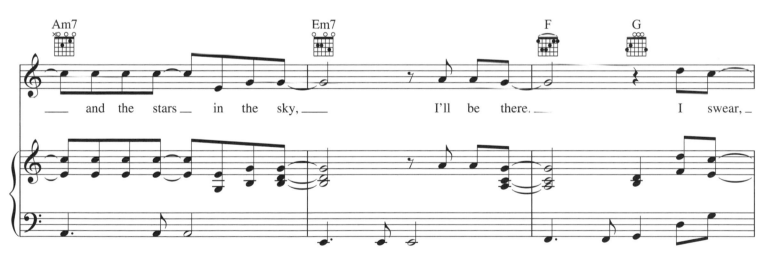

For bet-ter or worse, __ till death do us part, _____ I'll

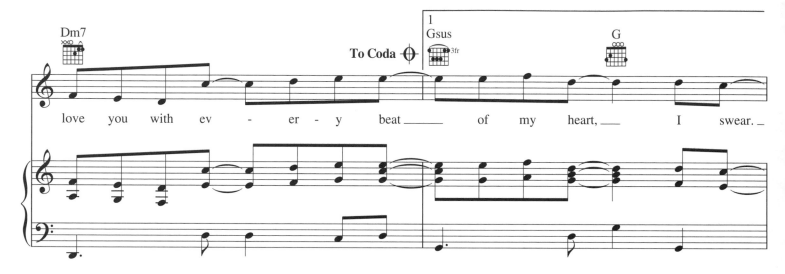

love you with ev-er-y beat _____ of my heart, ___ I swear. __

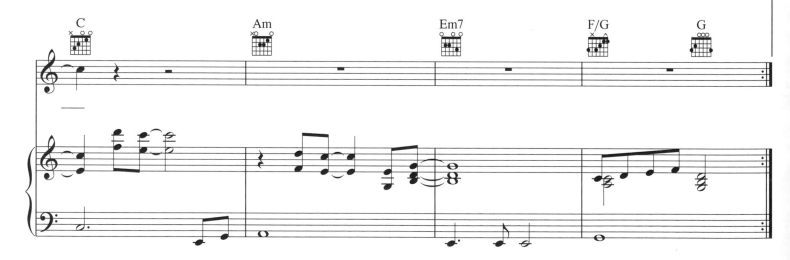

_____ of my heart, __ I swear. __ *Instrumental solo*

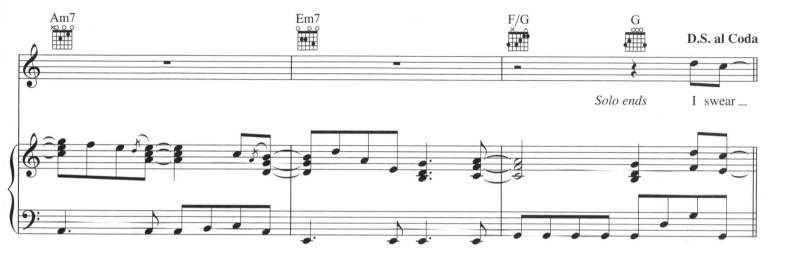

Solo ends   I swear __

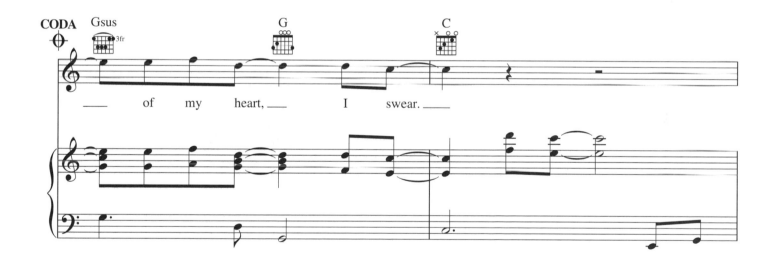

CODA

___ of my heart, ___   I swear. ____

I   swear. _____

HERE

Words and Music by STEVE ROBSON
and JEFFREY STEELE

There's a place _____ - ing

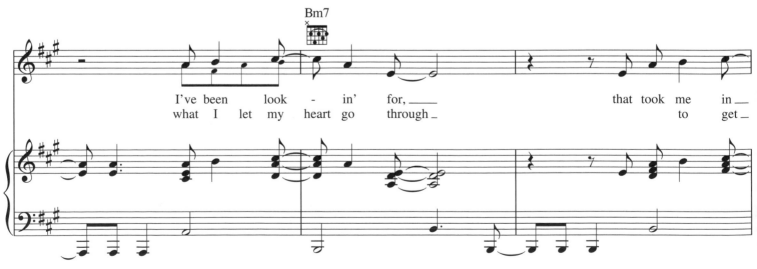

I've been look - in' for, _____ that took me in
what I let my heart go through _____ to get

16

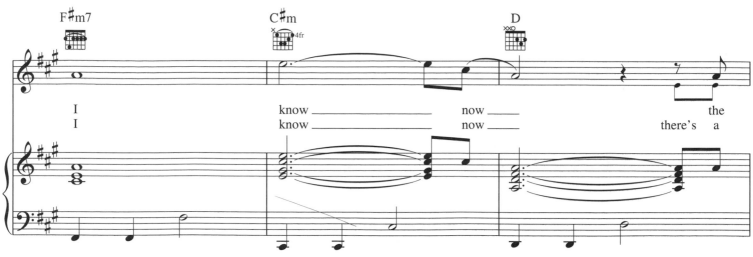

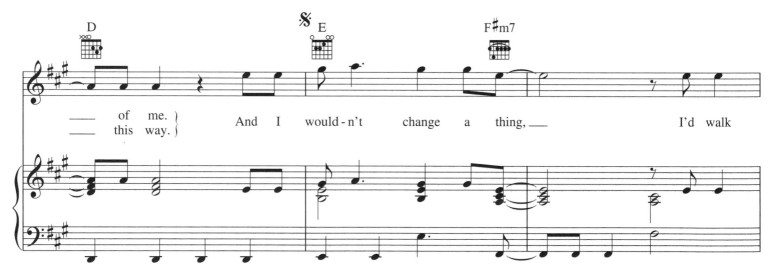

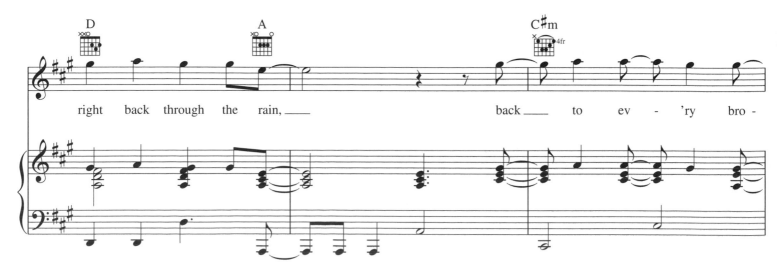

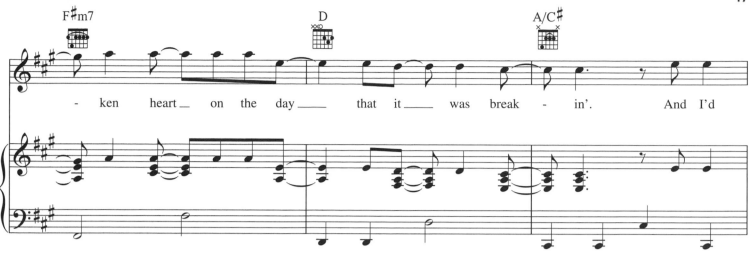

ken heart___ on the day___ that it___ was break - in'. And I'd

re - live all the years___ and be thank - ful for the tears___

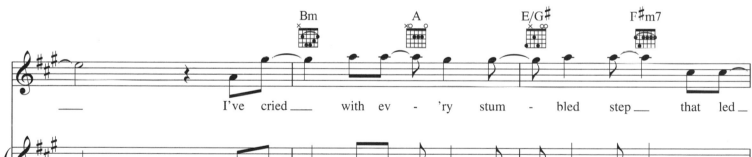

___ I've cried___ with ev - 'ry stum - bled step___ that led___

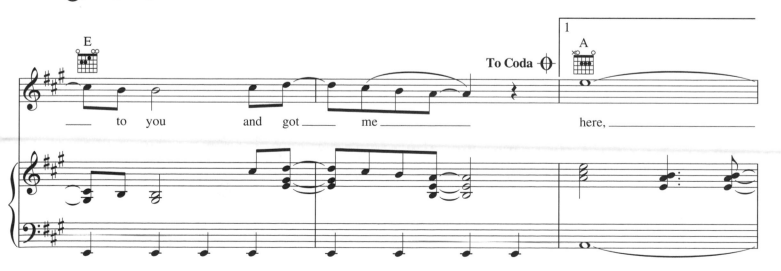

___ to you and got___ me___ here,___

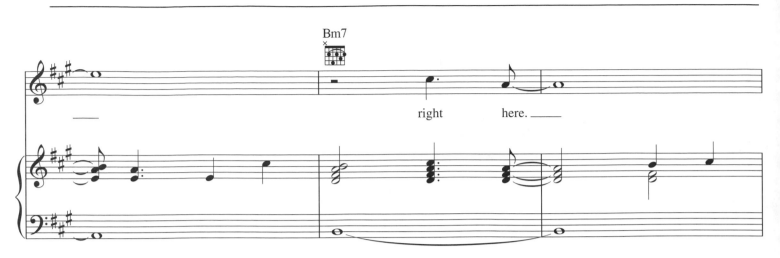

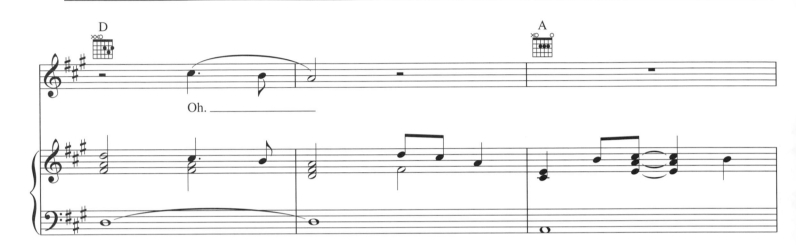

And if that's the road ___ God made me take ___ to be ___

___ with you... ___

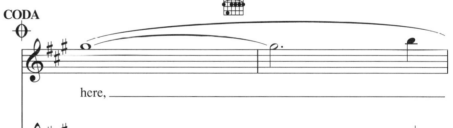

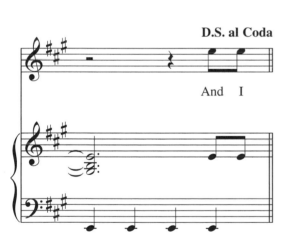

D.S. al Coda

And I

CODA

here, ___

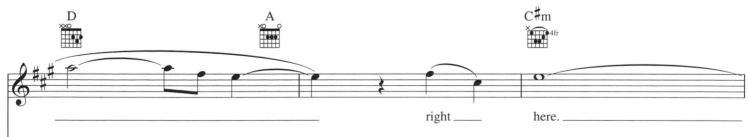

right ___ here. ___

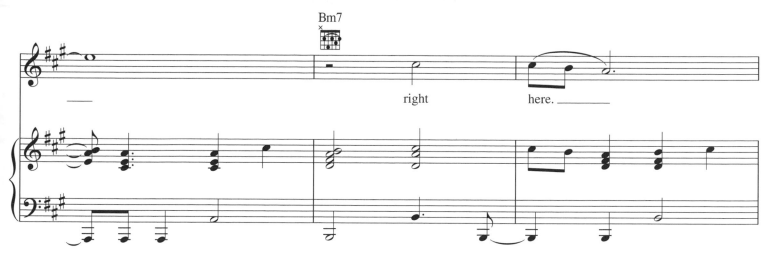

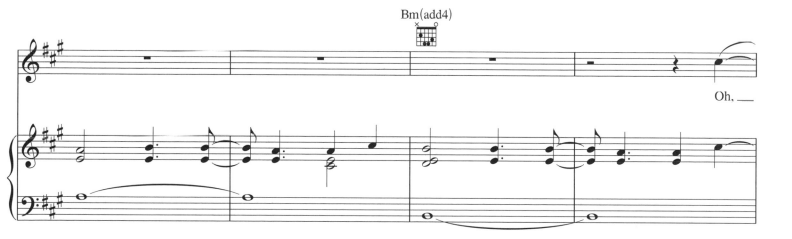

I NEED YOU

Words and Music by DENNIS MATKOSKY
and TY LACY

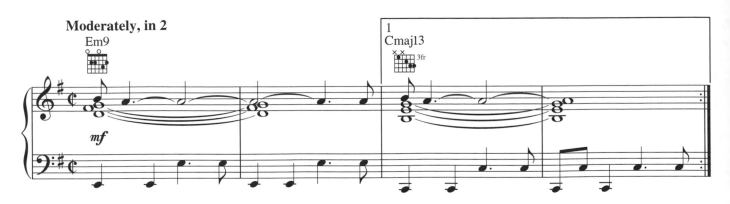

I don't need a lot____ of things; I can

*Vocal line written one octave higher than sung.

get by with noth - ing. Of all the bless - ings life

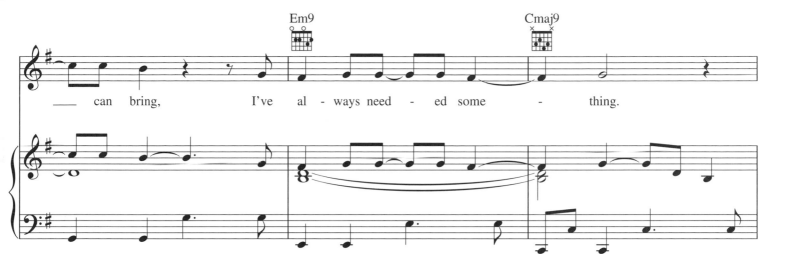

can bring, I've al - ways need - ed some - thing.

But I've got all I want when it comes to lov - ing You.

You're my on - ly rea - son,

24

You're my on - ly truth. I need___ You___ like wa -

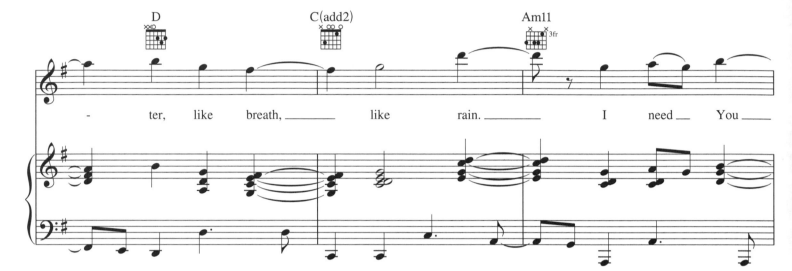

- ter, like breath,_____ like rain._____ I need___ You___

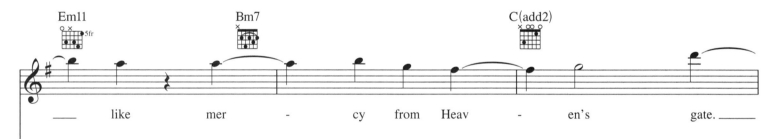

___ like mer - cy from Heav - en's gate.

There's a free - dom in___ Your___ arms___ that

car - ries me ____ through. ____ I need You. ____

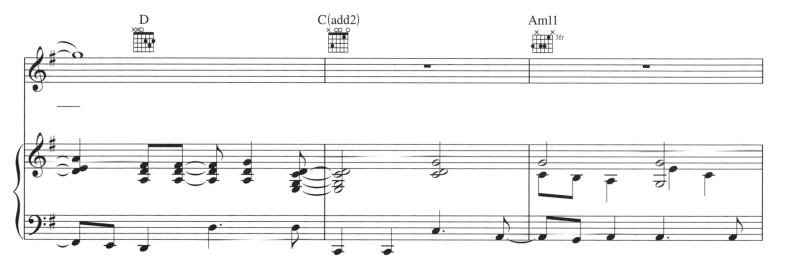

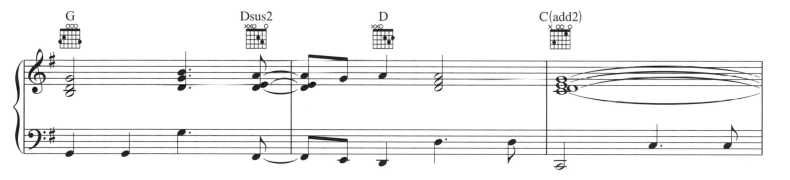

You're the hope that moves ____ me to

cour-age a-gain, _____ oh, yeah. _____ You're the love that res-

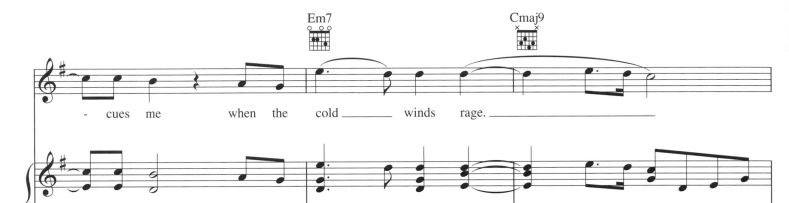

-cues me when the cold _____ winds rage. _____

And it's so a-maz-ing, 'cause that's just how You are. _____

_____ And I can't turn back _____ now, 'cause You've

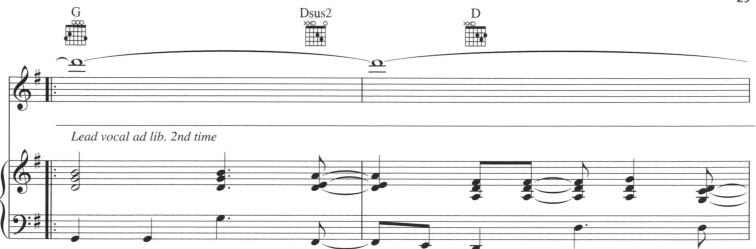

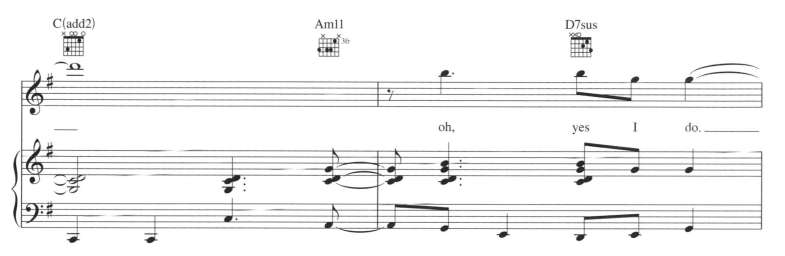

oh, yes I do. _____

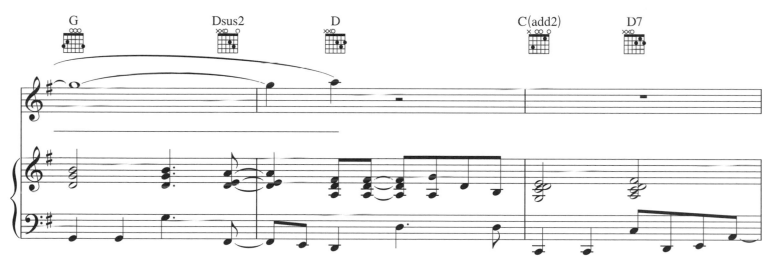

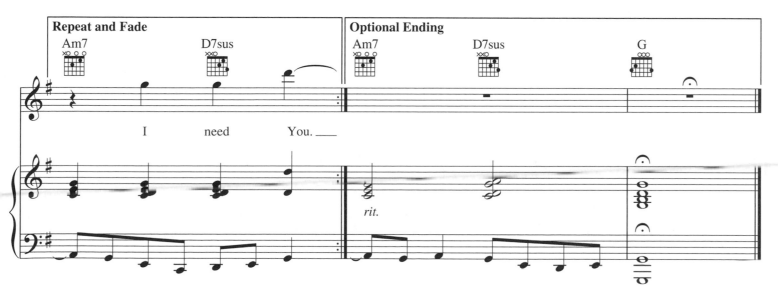

Repeat and Fade

I need You. ____

rit.

Optional Ending

IT'S YOUR LOVE

Words and Music by
STEPHONY E. SMITH

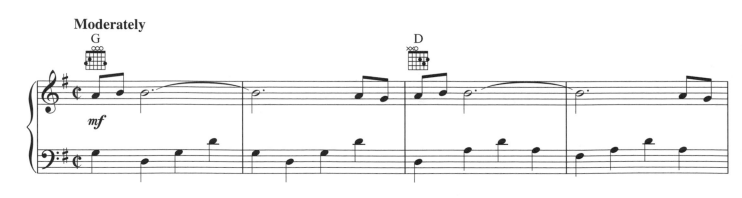

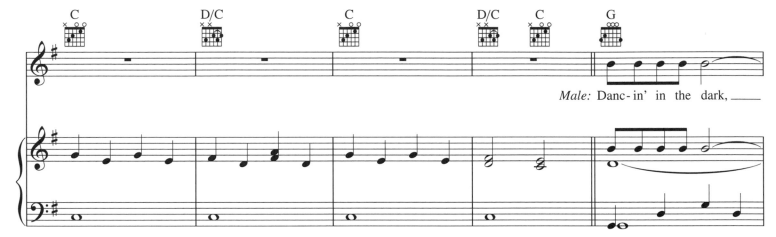

touch-in' my skin, and ask-in' you to do what

you've been do-in' all o-ver a-gain. Oh, it's a beau-ti-ful ___ thing. ___

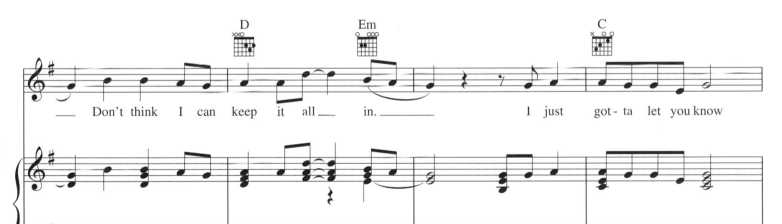

___ Don't think I can keep it all ___ in. ___ I just got-ta let you know

what it is that ___ won't let me go. *Both:* It's your love. ___ It just does some-thin'

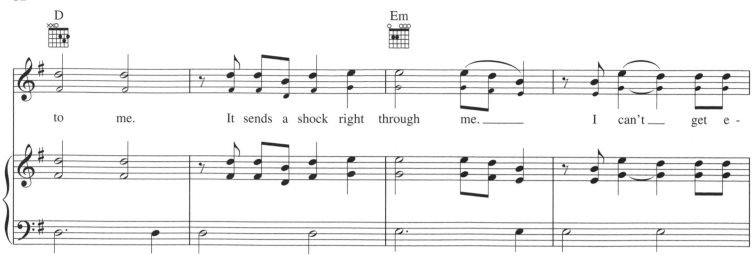

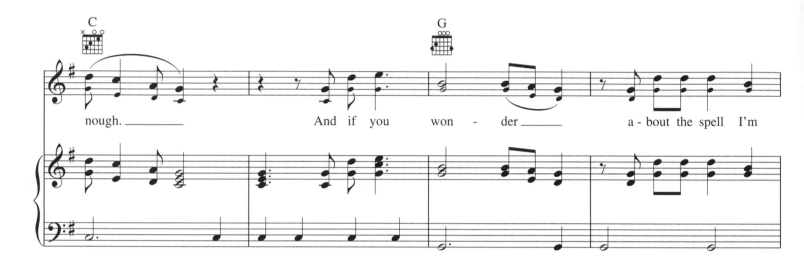

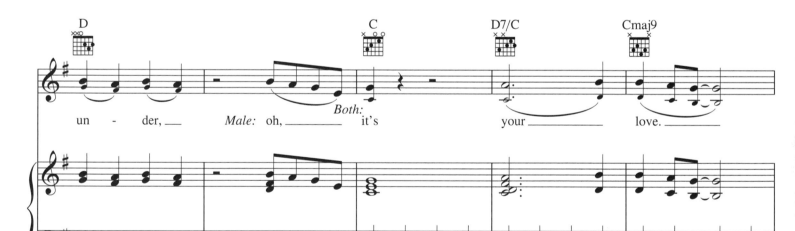

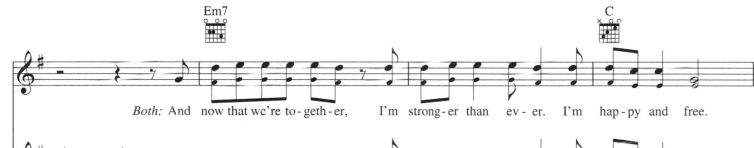

Male: Oh, did you ask me why I've changed? All I got-ta do is say your sweet name. _
Both: I just got-ta let you know what it is that won't let me go.

Both: It's your love. _____ It just does some-thin' to me. It sends a shock right

through me. _____ I can't ___ get e - nough. _____ And if you

won - der _____ a-bout the spell I'm un - der, ___ *Male:* oh, _____ it's

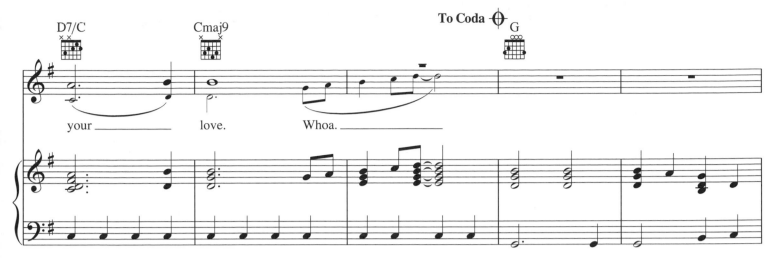

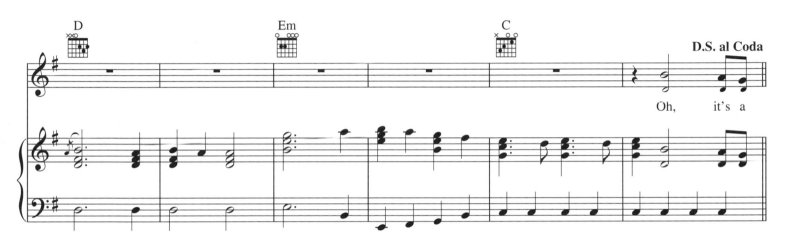

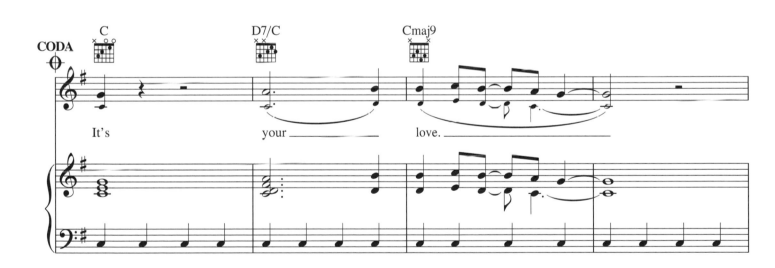

THE KEEPER OF THE STARS

Words and Music by KAREN STALEY,
DANNY MAYO and DICKEY LEE

Moderate Ballad

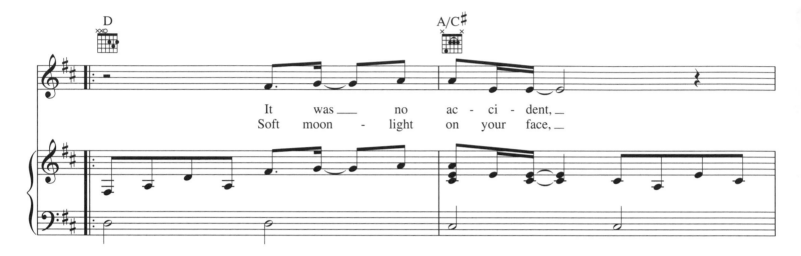

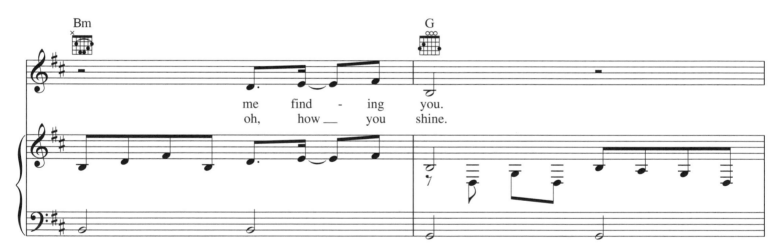

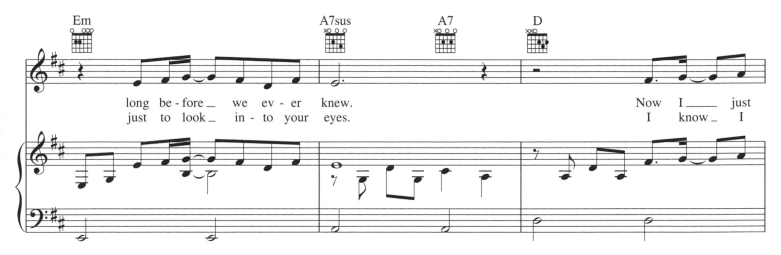

long be-fore ___ we ev-er knew.
just to look ___ in-to your eyes.

Now I ___ just
I know ___ I

can't ___ be - lieve ___
don't ___ de - serve ___

you're in ___ my
a treas - ure ___ like

life.
you.

Heav - en's smil - in'
There real - ly ___

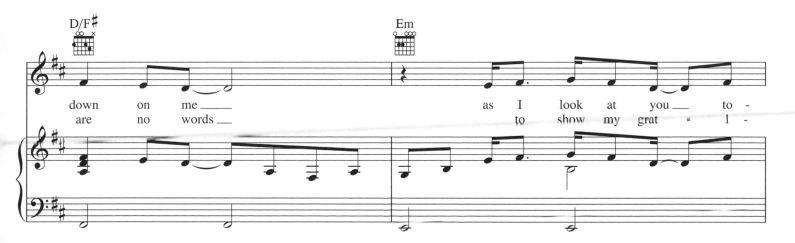

down on me ___
are no words ___

as I look at you ___ to-
to show my grat - i -

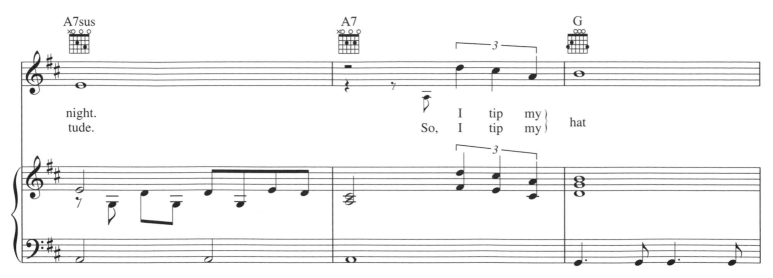

night.
tude.

So, I tip my hat

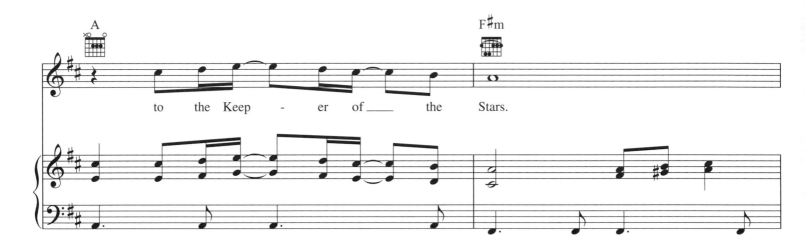

to the Keep - er of ___ the Stars.

He sure knew what he ___ was do - in' ___

when he joined these two hearts.

I hold ev - 'ry -

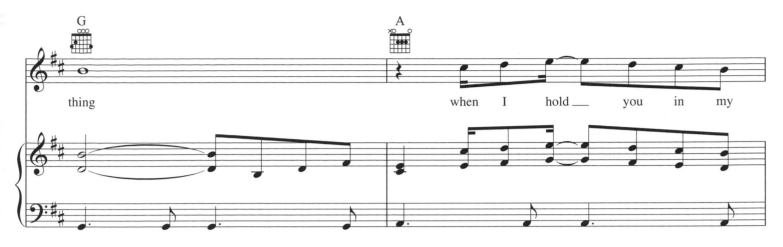

thing

when I hold ___ you in my

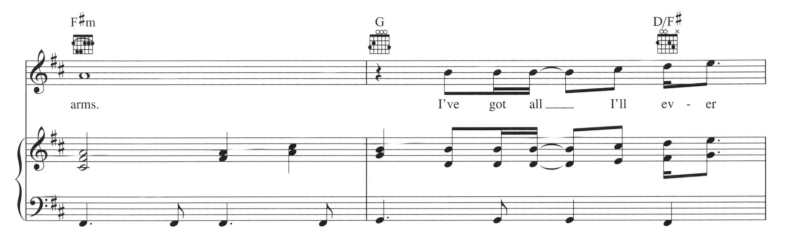

arms.

I've got all ___ I'll ev - er

need,

thanks to the Keep - er of ___ the

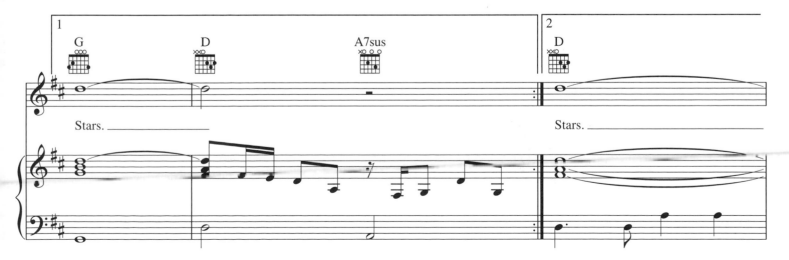

Stars. _____

Stars. _____

It was_ no ac - ci - dent,_

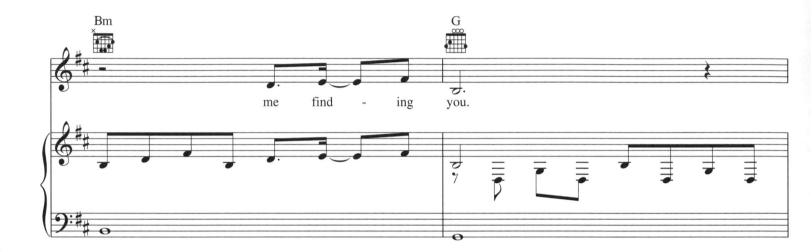

me find - ing you.

Some - one had a hand in it_

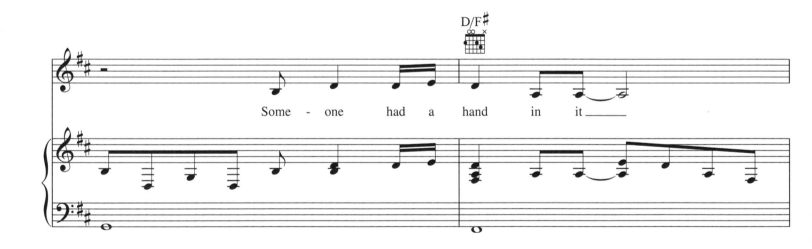

long be - fore_ we ev - er knew.

rit.

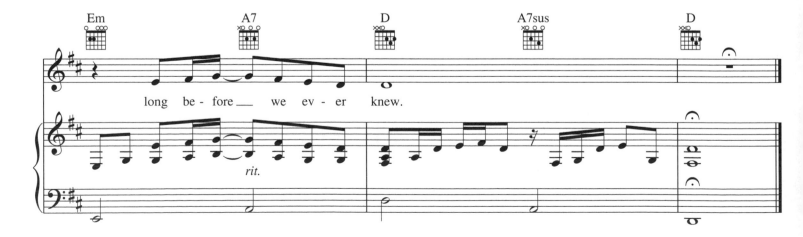

THEN

Words and Music by ASHLEY GORLEY,
BRAD PAISLEY and CHRIS DUBOIS

Moderately

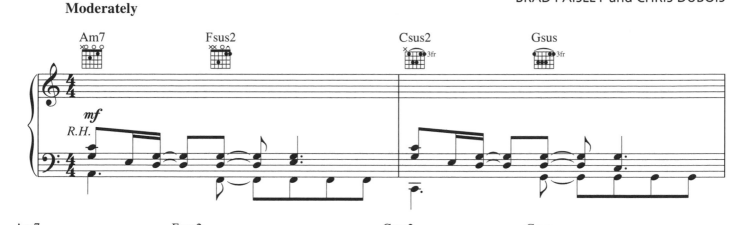

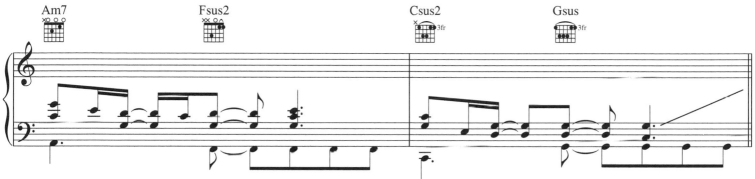

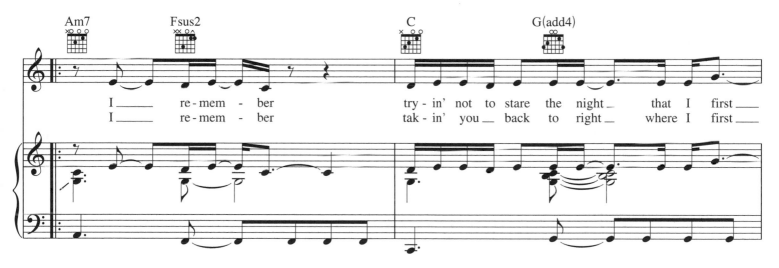

I ____ re-mem-ber ____ try-in' not to stare the night ____ that I first ____
I ____ re-mem-ber ____ tak-in' you ____ back to right ____ where I first ____

____ met you. You had me mes-mer-ized. ____ And
____ met you. You were so sur-prised. ____ There were

three weeks lat-er in the front porch light, tak-in' for-ty-five min-utes to kiss good-night. _ I had-n't
peo-ple a-round, _ but I did-n't care. _ I got down _ on one knee _ right there, _ and

told you yet, _ but I thought I loved you then. _
once a-gain, _ I thought I loved you then. _

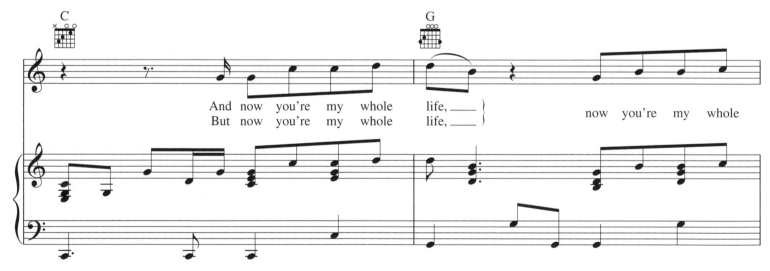

And now you're my whole life, _
But now you're my whole life, _

now you're my whole

world, _ and I just can't _ be-lieve _ the way I feel a-bout _ you, girl. _

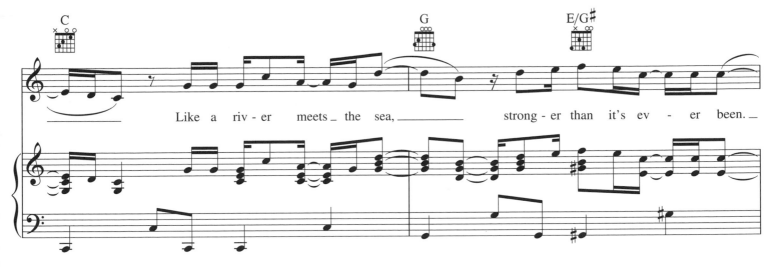

Like a riv-er meets _ the sea, _____ strong-er than it's ev - er been. __

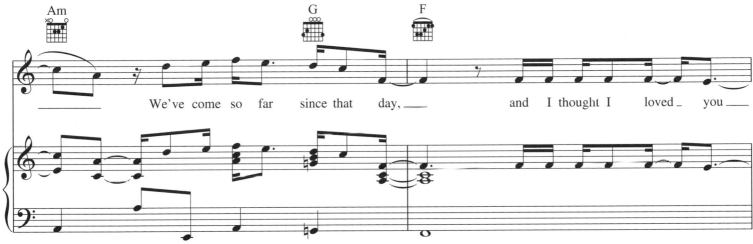

_____ We've come so far since that day, ___ and I thought I loved _ you __

1

__ then. _____

2

__ then. _____

But I've said that __ be - fore. __

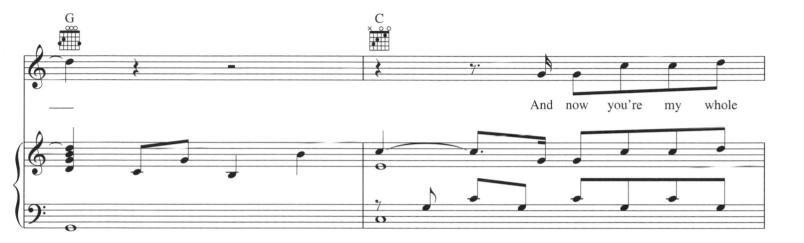

And now you're my whole

life, __ now you're my whole world, __ and I just can't __ be - lieve __

__ the way __ I feel __ a - bout __ you, girl. __ We'll look back __ some - day __

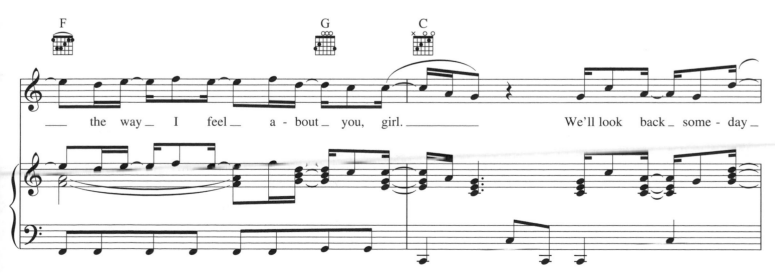

at this mo-ment that __ we're in, _____ and I'll look at you __ and

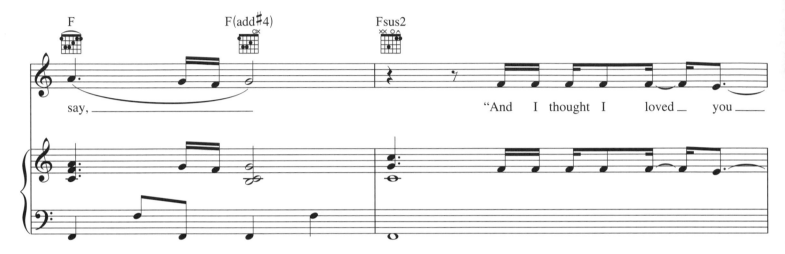

say, _____ "And I thought I loved __ you __

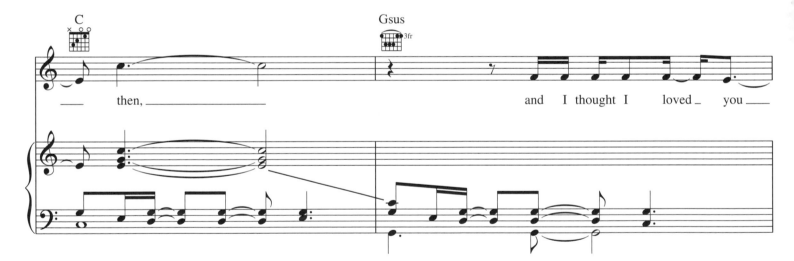

__ then, _____ and I thought I loved __ you __

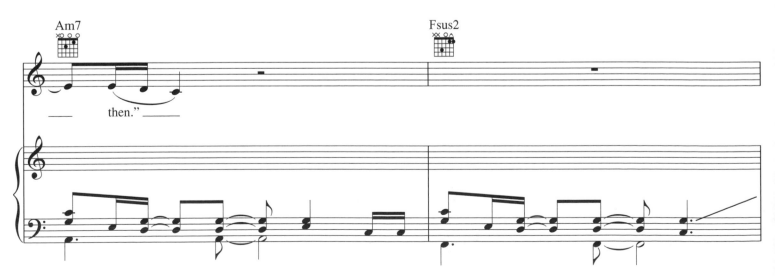

__ then." _____

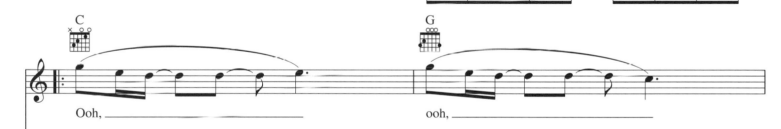

LOVE REMAINS

Words and Music by TOM DOUGLAS
and JIM DADDARIO

way.
side.
you.

Ma - ma smiles, _____ Tears _____ and sweat,
We _____ all live

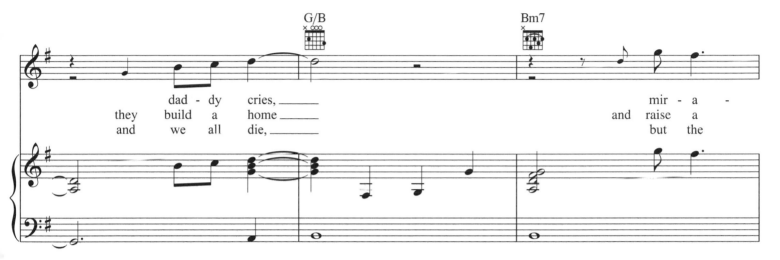

dad - dy cries, _____
they build a home _____
and we all die, _____

mir - a -
and raise a
but the

cle _____
fam - i - ly
end _____

be - fore their eyes.
of their own.
is not good - bye.

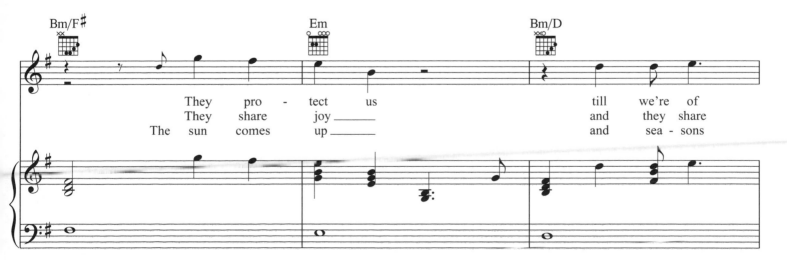

They pro - tect us
They share joy _____
The sun comes up _____

till we're of
and they share
and sea - sons

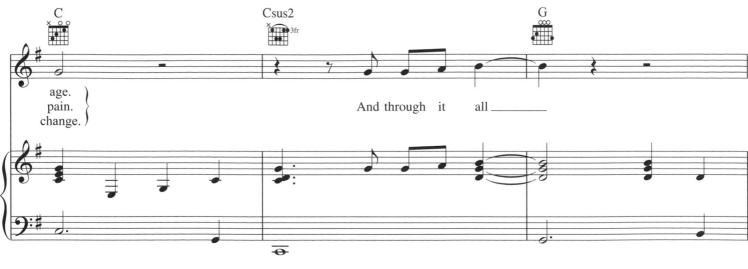

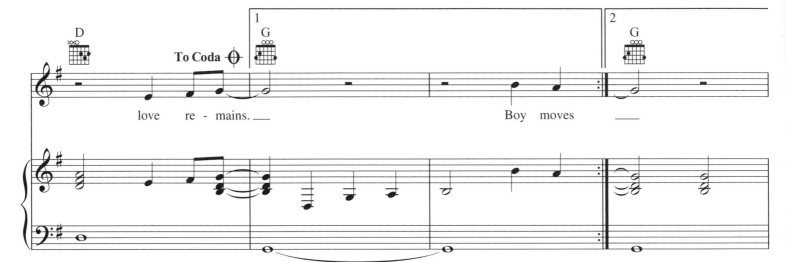

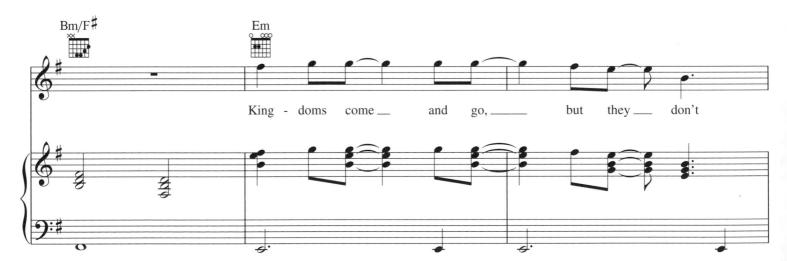

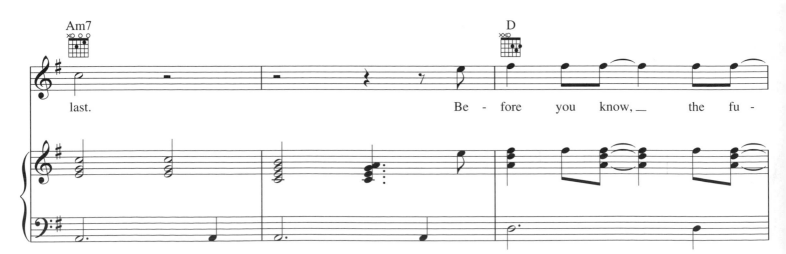

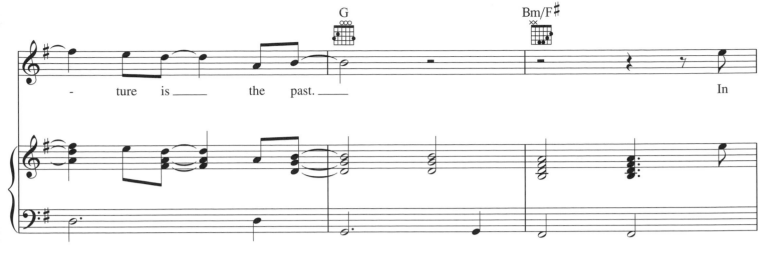

-ture is ___ the past. ___ In

spite of what's _ been lost ___ or what's _ been gained,

we are liv - ing proof ___ that

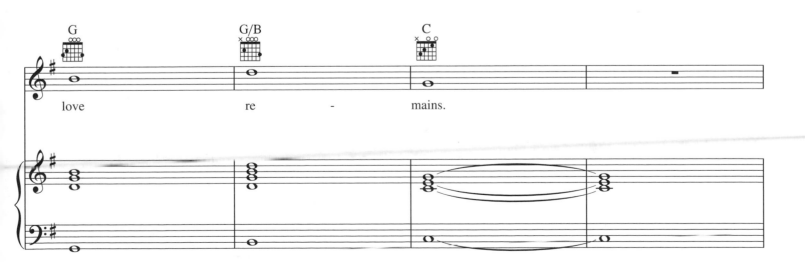

love re - mains.

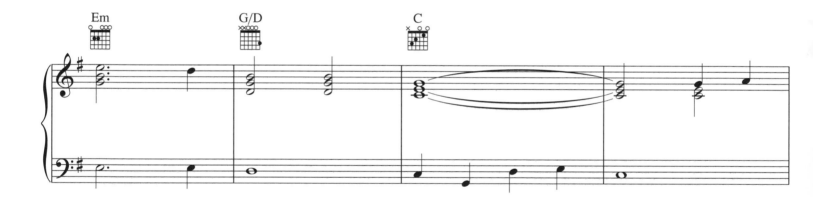

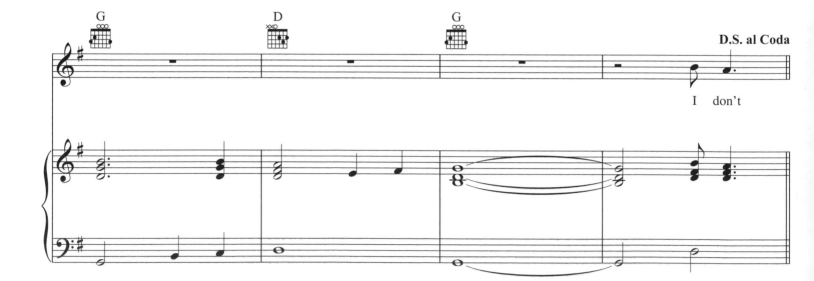

D.S. al Coda

I don't

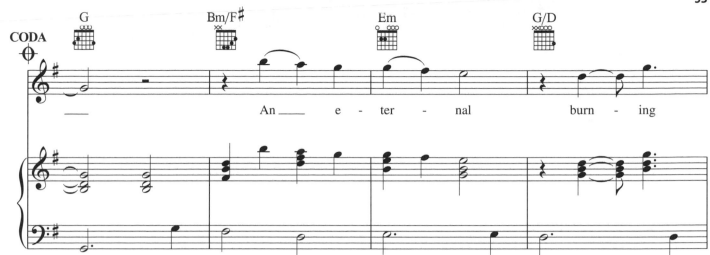

An ___ e - ter - nal burn - ing

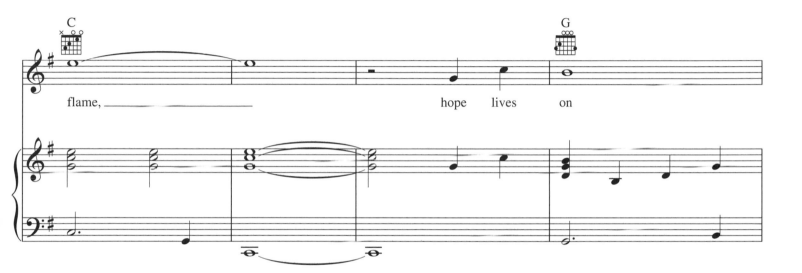

flame, ___ hope lives on

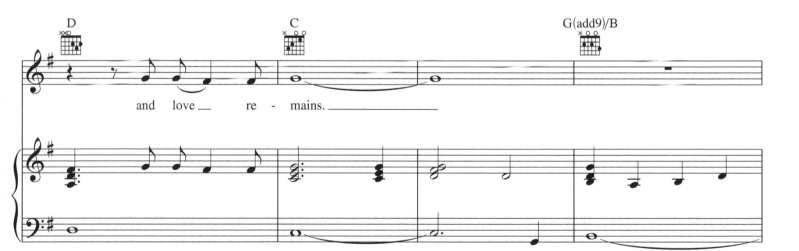

and love ___ re - mains. ___

rit.

THROUGH THE YEARS

Words and Music by STEVE DORFF
and MARTY PANZER

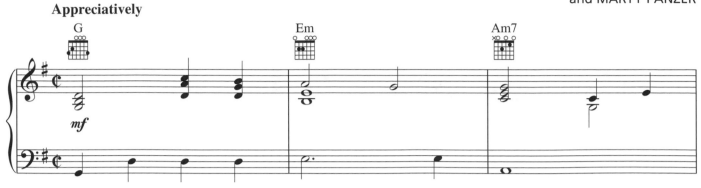

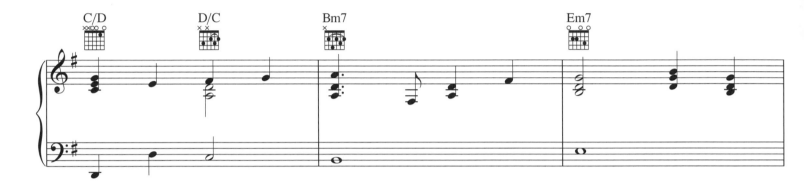

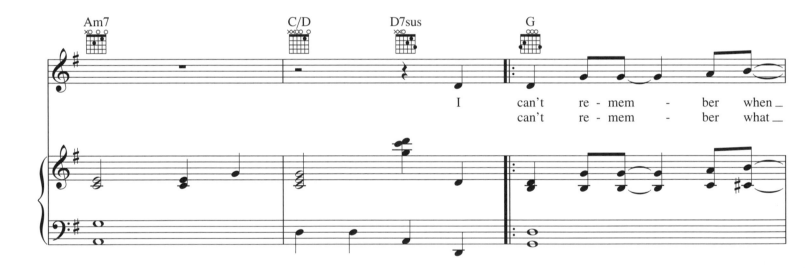

I can't re - mem - ber when _
can't re - mem - ber what _

_ you were - n't there, _ when I did - n't care
_ I used _ to do, _ who I trust - ed, who _

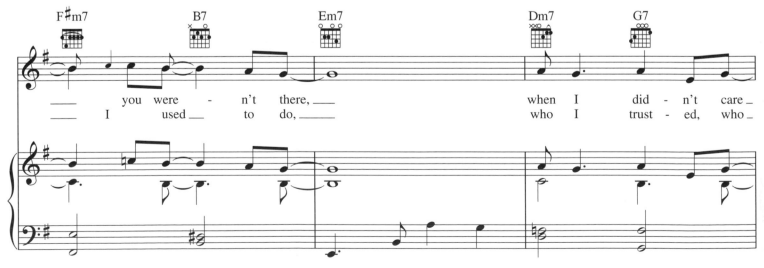

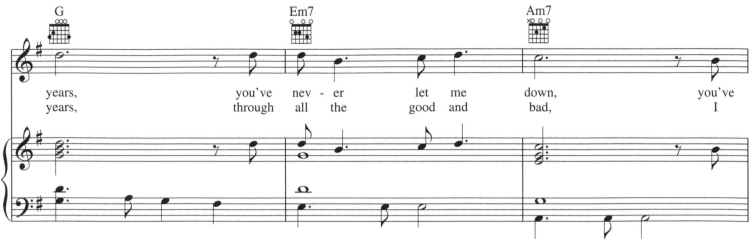

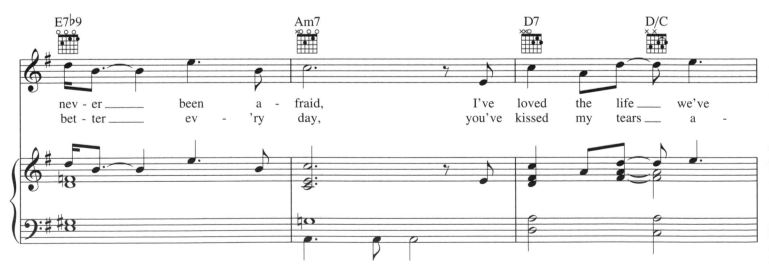

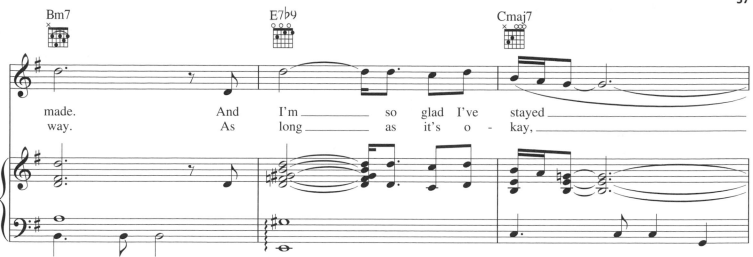

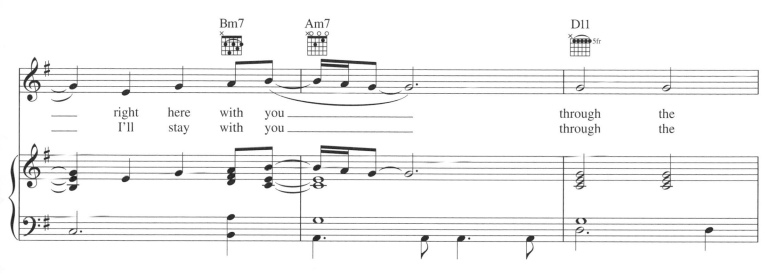

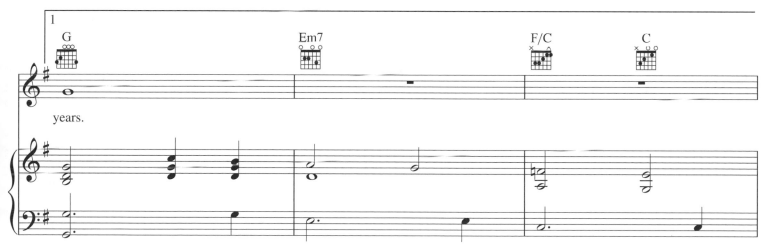

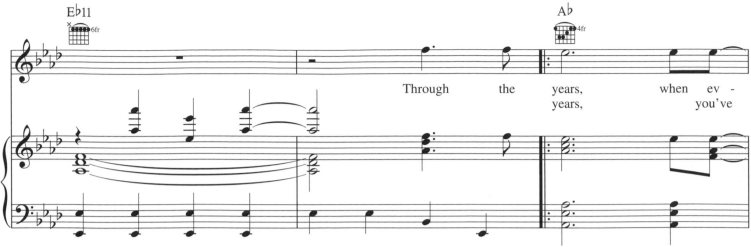

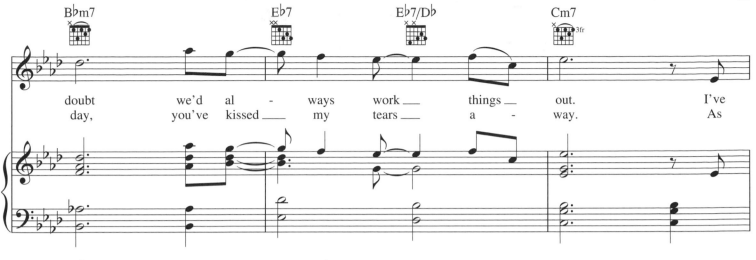

doubt, we'd al - ways work __ things __ out.
day, you've kissed __ my tears __ a - way.
I've
As

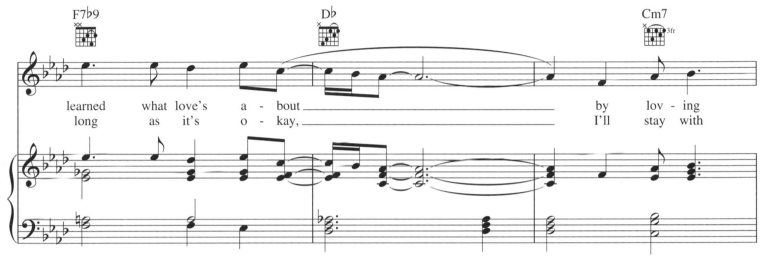

learned what love's a - bout _____ by lov - ing
long as it's o - kay, _____ I'll stay with

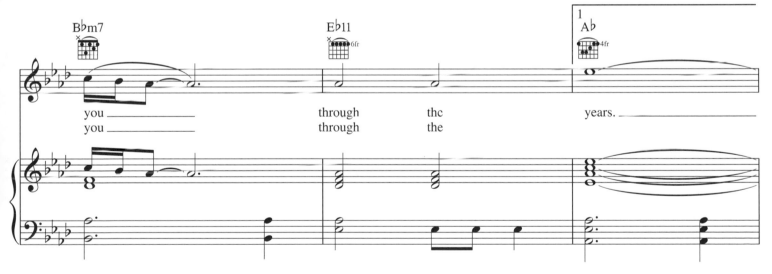

you _____
you _____
through the years.
through the

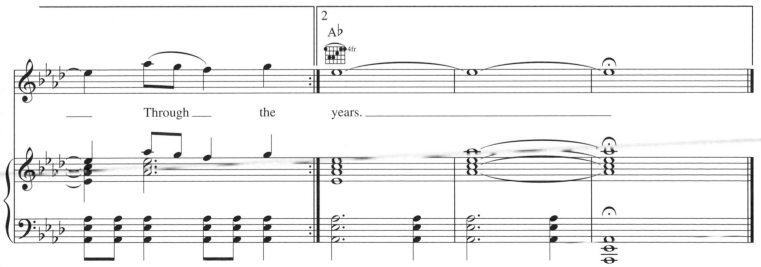

Through __ the years. _____

WHEN YOU SAY NOTHING AT ALL

Words and Music by DON SCHLITZ
and PAUL OVERSTREET

Moderately slow

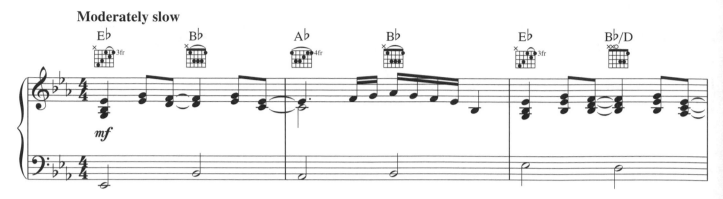

It's a-maz-ing how you can speak right to my heart.
All day long I can hear peo-ple talk-ing out loud,

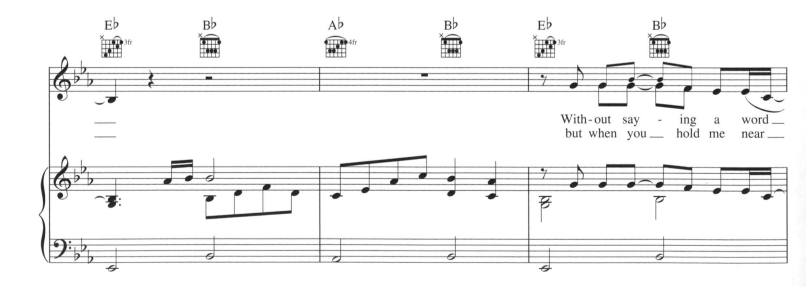

With-out say-ing a word
but when you hold me near

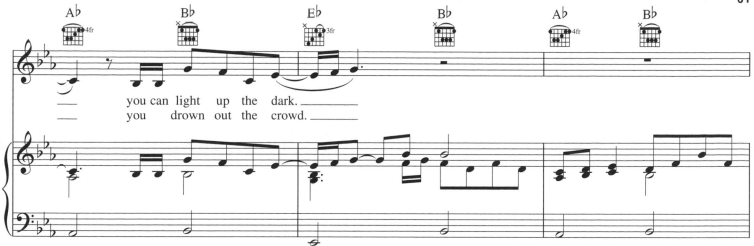

you can light up the dark. _____
you drown out the crowd. _____

Try as I may _____ I could nev - er ex - plain _____
Old Mis - ter Web - ster could nev - er de - fine _____

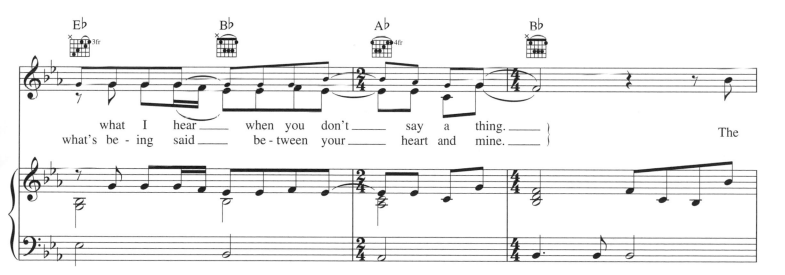

what I hear _____ when you don't _____ say a thing. _____ }
what's be - ing said _____ be - tween your _____ heart and mine. _____ }

The

smile on your face _____ lets me know _____ that you need _____ me. There's a

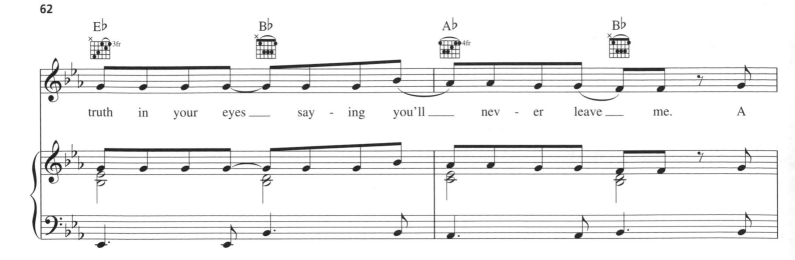

truth in your eyes __ say - ing you'll __ nev - er leave __ me. A

touch of your hand __ says you'll catch __ me if ev - er I fall. __

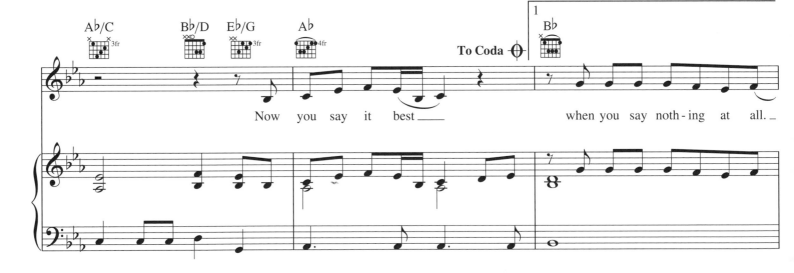

Now you say it best __ when you say noth - ing at all. __

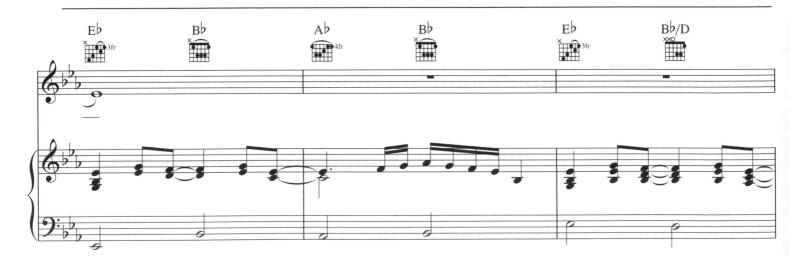

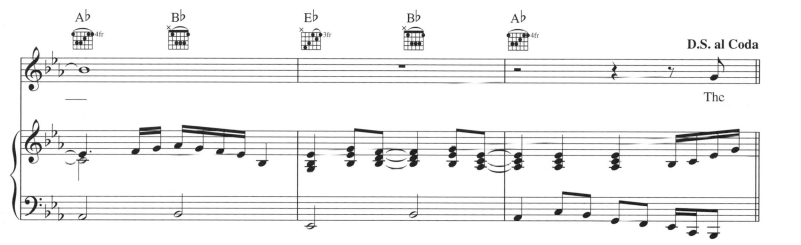

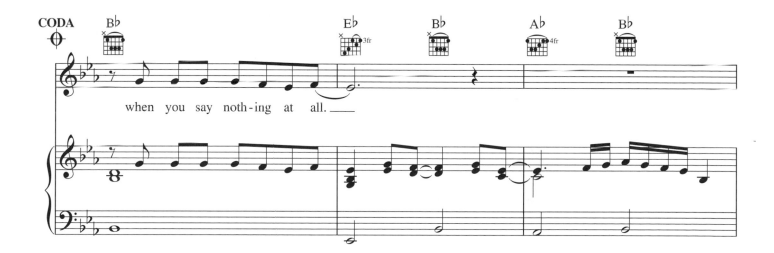

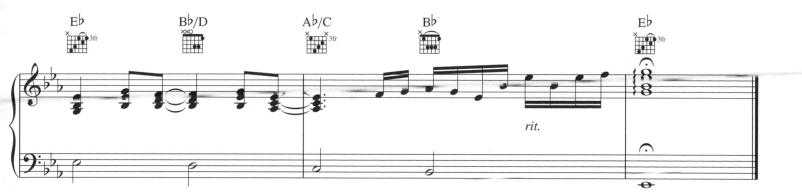

HAL•LEONARD
WEDDING ESSENTIALS

INCLUDES FULL PERFORMANCE CD

The Wedding Essentials series is a great resource for wedding musicians, featuring beautiful arrangements for a variety of instruments. Each book includes a reference CD to help couples choose the perfect songs for their wedding ceremony or reception. The CD is playable on any CD player, and is also enhanced so Mac and PC users can adjust the recording to any tempo without changing the pitch!

Christian Wedding Favorites
Answered Prayer • God Causes All Things to Grow • God Knew That I Needed You • Household of Faith • I Will Be Here • If You Could See What I See • Love Will Be Our Home • Seekers of Your Heart • This Day • 'Til the End of Time.
00311941 P/V/G.. $16.99

Contemporary Wedding Ballads
Beautiful in My Eyes • Bless the Broken Road • Endless Love • (Everything I Do) I Do It for You • From This Moment On • Have I Told You Lately • Here and Now • Love of a Lifetime • More Than Words • When You Say You Love Me.
00311942 P/V/G.. $16.99

Love Songs for Weddings
Grow Old with Me • Here, There and Everywhere • If • Longer • Part of My Heart • Valentine • We've Only Just Begun • The Wedding Song • You and I • You Raise Me Up.
00311943 Piano Solo... $16.99

Service Music for Weddings
PROCESSIONALS, RECESSIONALS, LIGHTING OF THE UNITY CANDLE
Allegro maestoso • Amazing Grace • Ave Maria • Canon in D • Jesu, Joy of Man's Desiring • Jupiter (Chorale Theme) • O Perfect Love • Ode to Joy • Rondeau • Trumpet Voluntary.
00311944 Piano Solo... $14.99

Wedding Guitar Solos
All I Ask of You • Gabriel's Oboe • Grow Old with Me • Hallelujah • Here, There and Everywhere • More Than Words • Sunrise, Sunset • Wedding Song (There Is Love) • When I Fall in Love • You Raise Me Up.
00701335 Guitar Solo.. $16.99

Wedding Vocal Solos
Grow Old with Me • I Swear • In My Life • Longer • The Promise (I'll Never Say Goodbye) • Someone Like You • Sunrise, Sunset • Till There Was You • Time After Time • We've Only Just Begun.
00311945 High Voice... $16.99
00311946 Low Voice... $16.99

Worship for Weddings
Be Unto Your Name • Broken and Beautiful • Center • He Is Here • Here and Now • Holy Ground • How Beautiful • Listen to Our Hearts • Today (As for Me and My House).
00311949 P/V/G.. $16.99

FOR MORE INFORMATION, SEE YOUR LOCAL MUSIC DEALER, OR WRITE TO:

HAL•LEONARD® CORPORATION
7777 W. BLUEMOUND RD. P.O. BOX 13819 MILWAUKEE, WI 53213
www.halleonard.com
Prices, content, and availability subject to change without notice.